Cricut (

Guide

The Ultimate Guide To Cricut Machines, Cricut Design Space, Cricut Project Ideas And Cricut Air Explore 2 For Beginners

Kelly J. White

Table Of Contents

Introduction

Thank you for purchasing this book.

Cricut has a sharper blade with smoother cutting edges, more consistent blade-to-blade contact, and less vibration than ever. Simply put, CRICUT delivers precision cuts in no time.

As the pandemic occurs, we all have limited ways of self-expression. Not many can go out for artistic pursuits; Cricut is one of the hobbies, a home tool for design, and even a business investment. This machine is easy to use and versatile for producing different types of paper.

Enjoy.

CHAPTER 1.

LEARN HOW TO WORK WITH COLOR

There are three possible ways to configure the color in an image or object in space design Cricut:

•   Basic color section

•   Custom Color Selector

•   Hex values

Imagine having an inserted image in the magnified view, but you have to change the color of the layer. To do this, click the layer button on the right side of the screen. You should be able to see the option line type, where you can see the primary colors (must be 30 primary colors), the selector custom color, you can use the mouse to go up and down the stopper for the color you want, or if you are familiar with hexadecimal values, you can enter the amount you wish to in that window. Sounds simple, right?

Printing and Cutting

Strange as it may seem, this machine can print the final version of your project and submit the project to be cut on your Cricut machine. Your laptop or computer is already connected to the printer, so why not print the project completed in their printers? This is why Machine Design Space has the Print option than cut it. You may even prepare the process, passing through printing. Then, cut calibration. For this procedure, follow these steps.

Open space design Cricut, go to the Account menu, and select Print, then cut calibration. After that, the window appears for this operation. Put the calibration sheet printed on the cutting, placing it in the mat's upper left corner. Simply click Continue. Make sure the Cricut machine is on and connected to your computer or laptop (via USB or Bluetooth), and select the device from the drop-down menu. The next step is choosing the right material adjustment, place the plate on the machine, and press Go on the computer.

You do not have to download the table, but will have to check if the cut plays the printed line. Doing so in the design space, you will need to click Yes and then click Continue to get to the next step.

The machine will start the calibration process cutting along the top and side of the page. When finished, do not download the table, but take a closer look at the lines along the sides and the top of the page. Perhaps, some do not touch the printed copy, but maybe others will. The space design software will ask you which letters and numbers cuts are closer than half of the printed lines.

To choose the number of the line that is closer to the centerline, click Start and to select the letter that is closer to the centerline, right-click. When finished, click Continue.

At this point, the machine will make a cut confirmation box around the leaf. When this is done, you can download the mat, remove the calibration sheet, and check the last question in the design space. If you are satisfied with the court, tick yes, then keep getting information to the final calibration screen. Click Save and Close to save the calibration settings.

You are ready and ready to go.

CHAPTER 2

YOU CAN CREATE BUSINESS OPPORTUNITIES

The creativity of your designs and the skill you will develop can allow you to create and start your own business if you wish. For enthusiastic novices, many questions would be faced, such as:

1. Where Do I Start?

Like any start-up business, initial questions need to be addressed to overcome possible difficulties. For example, addressing issues like defining my clientele, the products that might be of interest, where to find them, and how to make a profit margin of my sales are important to tackle from the start. In other words, you will need a good and well-defined business strategy to start with.

2. Choosing My Clientele

You can target two avenues to sell your products: either by looking at how you can approach the market locally or online. It is advisable to concentrate efforts on one approach to start with as your target is to generate profits as soon as possible. Never forget that your goal is to grow benefits and reinvest it, so that your business expands. The quicker you increase your sales, the more likely you will reinvest in new tools or new products, making, in turn, a stronger financial turnover. Understanding your marketing strategy is the key to your success.

3. Approaching Local Markets

You can explore selling your products from 'business to business.' In this configuration, the volume of sales is of importance as the larger the production, the lower the production cost per item is. This is the most challenging balance to reach for a new Cricut-based business. The advantage of obtaining contractual work means you can negotiate to buy a large quantity from vendors. However, such 'golden' opportunities are hard to find since such contracts are opened to competition. Yet, as a new start-up business, you can present your products specifically tailored for business customers. A custom work approach offers positive aspects as businesses always look for originality and good products. By creating such a relationship, your business is likely to become a point of reference for future other contacts, hence launching many upselling opportunities.

Another approach to consider for selling your products is from 'business to customer.' In this model, though the sales volume remains important, your objective is to present your products to retail customers willing to buy them. Creativity, imagination will be the keys to your success, as well as what type of media and medium you want to work in (e.g., T-shirts, mugs). Equally important is a retail space you will need to choose to offer your items. Experiencing different locations and products is all part of the efforts of a new start-up business. A custom work approach for local customers will also present advantages since the start-up costs are the lowest of all the different strategies described so far. However, as a new business in the field, starting can be difficult. Word of mouth can be your first step, and produce good products at an affordable price.

4. Selling Online

If you are adept at higher technical knowledge, you can generate great benefits by providing quality custom work, bulk offering, or information network. If you choose, for example, a custom work approach, you increase the chances to find potential customers looking for your products as they turn to a search engine like Google to find what they are looking for. Websites like Amazon Handmade, or Etsy provide a good platform to allow to sell custom design services. Equally efficient is the launch of your site. This strategy is worth looking at. Selling online presents advantages such as low start-up costs and access to the global market with millions of potential customers.

Furthermore, online custom prices tend to be lower than those on the local market. However, access to the global market means that competition is stiff, pushing products competitively. Selling online requires certain knowledge in logistics as far as shipping and packing your products are concerned, a cost factor that needs to be considered in your pricing.

If you prefer to sell your products online through information networks, then you become an authority in the field, creating the opportunity to generate profit with your Cricut designs. By offering blogs on technical know-how or inspiration work, you become selective on the posts you want to take on.

Starting a new business requires foremost a business strategy, the foundation for your future success. Asking yourself who your potential customers would be, what kind of products you can sell them, and how are the first steps of a future startup business.

CHAPTER 3

BECOME AN EXPERT USING CRICUT DESIGN SPACE

Technique

One of the biggest things you'll find that will help you to pull off the perfect project is patience. You will find that if you relax, take your time to goad the material into doing what it should, think of creative solutions, and you will find a greater success rate in your projects with the Cricut system. Always go into your projects with a can-do attitude, a quizzical mindset, and a lot of patience. You will find your projects roll by much more smoothly and are more fun when you do it this way!

In our Tips & Tricks section of this chapter, you will find more specifics on ways in which to improve the quality of the crafts you create and ways in which to do so more easily! We'll have a lot of information on extending the life of your accessories and materials, as well as ways to use the most economically!

Tips & Tricks for Efficient and Easier Cricut Use

Harbor Freight is a Good Resource

Harbor Freight has sets of hooks that are similar to the weeding tool that Cricut has to offer. These sets of weeding hooks generally run very cheap, and so the job just as well as Cricut's proprietary weeding hooks. If you find that this is a tool you use may need to replace often, consider looking at Harbor Freight or another hardware retailer for a suitable replacement on a budget and in bulk!

Adhere Your Materials to Your Mats with Painter's or Masking Tape

You will find that, as your Cricut mats age, they will slowly lose their grip. Before completely giving up on your mat and throwing it out, considering lining the edges of your project with painter's tape or with masking tape. This will hold your materials in place while they're being cut and will save you the expense of a new mat for some time.

Having a mat with a fresh, strong grip is invaluable, and it makes your projects go by so much more quickly. However, the realists among us know that it's not always feasible to dash out to the crafting store and drop some money on craft mats when there are bills to be paid! Painter's tape or masking tape is a great stopgap in just such an event.

Command Hooks from 3M to Hang Your Cutting Mats When Not in Use

Utilizing your wall space for storage can be invaluable when you're storing something that is delicate and prone to bending, like your Cricut craft mat. Using Command hooks will ensure that your walls won't be damaged by the adhesive, and your mats will always be within arm's reach and will never be hidden from you with this method!

Keep the Clear Plastic Sheet That Comes with Your Cricut Mats

When you buy a fresh Cricut mat, you will notice a semi-rigid sheet of plastic that comes stuck to the grip. After you complete each project, re-adhere this sheet to the front of your mat before hanging them up or putting them away! This will keep the grip from getting ruined by dust, hair, rogue glitter, or animal fur in the air!

Try Using Contact Paper as Transfer Tape

One hack that a number of craters, bloggers, and YouTubers swear by is buying contact paper from either Target or the Dollar Tree and using it at transfer tape! The adhesive on contact paper is meant to be removed after months or even years of use with little to no residue. This quality makes it a great substitute for transfer tape, which we rely on to keep all our project pieces exactly in place between the carrier sheet and our project materials!

Blades Getting Dull Too Soon? Run Foil Through Your Cricut!

A very popular Cricut trick in use is to stick a clean, fresh piece of foil to your Cricut mat and run it through with the blade you wish to sharpen. Running the blades through the thin metal helps revitalize their edges and give them a little extra staying power until it's time to buy replacements.

Another way to do this is to make a ball of foil, remove the blades from the housing, and stick them into the ball of foil several times until you notice a shine on the blade. This can give you a better idea of how sharpened your blades are becoming before you finish up with them, and it seems like a more sensible way to sharpen several blades in one sitting. Still, the reviews seem to be equally as positive as letting your machine do the work for you on one blade at a time.

Cut Slits in The Edges of Your Transfer Tape

If you're transferring a decal onto something round, like a cup or mug, you will find it much easier to lay the decal flat if you cut intermittent slits in the transfer tape. You will find this cut down on its reusability, but you will get more even, less bubbly designs on your products, more reliably.

Reverse Weeding

This is a technique that is best used on designs that have a lot of intricate or delicate letters or lines. The way it's done is, once you've run your vinyl through your Cricut machine, adhere the transfer tape to the front of that vinyl piece. Burnish it with your scraper tool, then remove the carrier sheet or backing from the vinyl.

From here, you will use your weeding tool to remove the blanks and excess vinyl that is around your design. This gives you the added benefit of the excess vinyl adhering to your weeding tool, making it easier to peel it away. Since your design's letters and lines have already been burnished to your transfer tape, they will more likely stay where you need them.

Once you're done removing the excess, you are ready to adhere your design to any surface you desire!

Use Baby Powder to Reveal Cut Lines

When using glitter iron-on material, it can be very difficult to see where the cut lines are, thanks to the light refraction off all the glitter pieces. By taking a very small amount of baby powder and brushing it onto the back of your vinyl piece, you can see where those cut lines are more easily, and peel away the excess to reveal your design! You will only need a very small amount to do this, and you will find that the baby powder doesn't inhibit the iron-on material's ability to stick to your products!

Use a Binder and Page Protectors for Storage

You will find that, as you amass scraps of vinyl, paper, foil, and more, it will be hard to keep your spare materials from getting lost, damaged, curled, or worse. However, this can be completely avoided with this $2 hack! Buy a 3-ring binder and some page protectors. Use those protectors as pockets for similar materials, or organize them by size or color, and you will find that your scraps are safe and ready to use at all times!

IKEA Grocery Bag Holders as Material Organizers

You will find that IKEA's grocery bag holders/dispensers are designed in such a way that they will beautifully hold several rolls of Cricut materials each! These cost only $2.99 each at IKEA, are safe for your walls, and will keep your materials aesthetically displayed while keeping them safe from wrinkling, crinkling, or worse!

No matter how cluttered your desk space gets, those rolls will always be perfectly safe up there on the wall!

Pegboard Tool Storage

You will notice that one of the handier features of the proprietary tools that Cricut offers is that they all have little holes on the ends of their handles! This makes them perfect candidates for pegboard storage! I'm sure the brilliant minds at Cricut know this and intend this.

Simply hanging a pegboard over your workspace can keep all your tools readily available, but it can also help prolong your tools' lives!

Keeping your tools in a box that gets moved regularly can cause the tools to bump into each other, dulling their points or chipping their handles. Hanging your tools above your workstation ensures you'll be able to find what you need at all times, your tools will stay pristine for longer, and you'll be able to look at your pretty tools at all times!

Remove Debris with a Lint Roller

This one sounds obvious, but it's a lifesaver. Taking a lint roller to your Cricut mats can save you a lot of trouble and can keep the grip strong on your mats. Over time, you will find that paper and fabric fibers, glitter, dust, and debris get stuck to the grip on your mats. This torpedoes the grip strength in no time flat! Since Cricut strongly urges against cleaning your mats, you must realize that you do this at your own risk. However, a large number of Cricut crafters have said that this little tip has saved them from having to buy a new mat for an extra couple of weeks at least.

Wipe Down Your Mats with Non-Alcohol Wipes

Since Cricut strongly urges against cleaning your mats, you must realize that you do this at your own risk. However, a large number of Cricut crafters have said that this little tip has saved them from having to buy a new mat for an extra couple of weeks at least.

Since this is against Cricut's suggestion, you must hold off on trying it until it seems like your mat may be near the end of its grip life, when you would be replacing it anyway. This is so that if you find these hacks don't work, or they do damage, you will have needed to buy a new one soon anyway!

Using baby wipes or non-alcohol wipes on your mats can remove things that are stuck in the grip of your mat, clear away dirt or paper leavings, and can give you back a couple of extra weeks of grip strength in your mats!

CHAPTER 4

OVERVIEW: WHAT CAN WE CREATE

With Cricut, the ideas for projects are so vast; you'll be amazed at how much you can do.

So, what are some ideas that could work for you? Here are a few that you can consider and some of the best project ideas for those stumped on where to begin!

Easy Projects

Custom Shirts

Custom shirts are incredibly easy. The beauty of this is, you can use the Cricut fonts or system options, and from there, you can simply print it on.

I like to use iron on vinyl because it's easy to work with. Just take your image and upload it into Design Space.

Then, go to the canvas and find the image you want. Once you've selected the image, you click on the whitespace that will be cut, remember to get the insides, too.

Ensure that you choose a cut image, not print from the cut image, and then place it on the canvas to your liking size.

Put the iron-on vinyl shiny side down, turn it on, and then select iron-on from the menu.

Choose to cut, and make sure you mirror the image. Once done, pull off the extra vinyl to remove the vinyl between the letters.

There you go! A simple shirt.

Vinyl Decals

Vinyl can also be used to make personalized items, such as water bottle decals. First, design the text, you can pretty much use whatever you want for this.

From here, create a second box and make an initial, or whatever design you want. Make sure that you resize this to fit the water bottle, as well.

From here, load your vinyl, and make sure that you use transfer tape on the vinyl itself once you cut it out. Finally, when you adhere the lettering to the bottle, go from the center and then push outwards, smoothing as you go.

It takes a bit, but there you have it, simple water bottles that children will love!

This is a wonderful, simple project for those of us who aren't really that artistically inclined but want to get used to making Cricut items.

Printable Stickers

Printable stickers are the next project.

This is super simple and fun for parents and kids.

The Explore Air 2 machine works best. With this one, you want the print, then cut feature, since it makes it much easier. To begin, go to Design Space and download images of ice cream or whatever you want, or upload images of your own.

You click on a new project, and on the left side that says images, you can choose the ones you like and insert more of these on there. From here, choose the image and flatten it since this will make it into one piece rather than just a separate file for each.

Resize as needed to make sure that they fit where you're putting them.

You can copy/paste each element until you're done.

Once ready, press saves, and then choose this as a print, then cut the image.

Make sure everything is good, then press continue, and from there, you can load the sticker paper into the machine.

Make sure to adjust this to the right setting, which for sticker paper is the vinyl set.

Put the paper into there and load them in, and when ready, the press goes, it will then cut the stickers as needed.

From there, take them out and decorate. You can use ice cream or whatever sticker image you want!

Personalized Pillows

Personalized pillows are another fun idea and are incredibly easy to make. To begin, you open up Design Space and choose a new project.

From here, select the icon at the bottom of the screen itself, choosing your font.

Type the words you want, and drag the text as needed to make it bigger. You can also upload images, too, if you want to create a huge picture on the pillow itself.

Now, you want to press the attach button for each box, so that they work together and both are figured when centered, as well.

You then press make it, and you want to turn to mirror on, since this will, again, be on iron-on vinyl.

From here, you load the iron-on vinyl with the shiny side down, then press continues, follow the prompts, and make sure it's not jammed in, either.

Let the machine work its magic with cutting, and from there, you can press the weeding tool to get the middle areas out.

Set your temperature on the easy press for the right settings, and then push it onto the material, ironing it on and letting it sit for 10 to 15 seconds. Let it cool, and then take the transfer sheet off.

There you have it! A simple pillow that works wonders for your crafting needs.

Cards!

Finally, cards are a great project idea for Cricut makers.

They're simple, and you can do the entire project with cardstock. To make this, you first want to open up Design Space, and from there, put your design in.

If you like images of ice cream, then use that. If you want to make Christmas cards, you can do that, too.

Basically, you can design whatever you want to on this. Now, you'll then want to add the text.

You can choose the font you want to use, and from there, write out the message on the card, such as "Merry Christmas."

At this point, instead of choosing to cut, you want to choose the right option, the Make it option. You don't have to mirror this, but check that your design fits properly on the cardstock itself.

When choosing material for writing, make sure you choose the cardstock.

From there, insert your cardstock into the machine, and then, when ready, you can press go, and the Cricut machine will design your card.

This may take a minute, but once it's done, you'll have a wonderful card in place. It's super easy to use.

Cricut cards are a great personalized way to express yourself, creating a one-of-a-kind, sentimental piece for you to gift to friends and family.

Medium Projects

Cricut Cake Toppers

Cricut cake toppers have a little bit of added difficulty because they require some precise scoring.

The Cricut maker is probably the best piece of equipment for the job, and here, we'll tell you how to do it. The scoring tool is your best bet since this will make different shapes even easier, as well. You will want to make sure you have cardstock and the cutting mat, along with a fine-point blade for cutting.

The tape is also handy for these.

First, go to Design Space and choose the rosettes you want.

Scoring shells are meant to create extra-deep score lines in materials to get the perfect fold.

The single wheel will make one crease, and the double wheel will make a parallel wheel that will crease, perfect for specialty items.

Plus, the double wheel is thicker, so it's easier to fold. Once you score everything, you remove it and replace the scoring wheel with the fine-point blade.

From here, you simply fold everything and just follow the line.

This should make the rosette, and you can then use contrasting centers and create many of these to form a nice backdrop.

Cricut Gift Bags

Next are gift bags. Remember to put the foil poster board face-down on the mat itself to help prevent the material from cracking and showing through to the white backdrop when you fold them together after you score them.

To make these, you want to implement the template you'd like to use in Design Space.

From here, I do suggest cutting out the initial design first and then putting it back in to create scoring lines, following the same steps.

After that, you can then take your item and fold it along the score lines, and then use adhesive or glue to help put it all together.

This is a great personalized way to do it but can be a bit complicated to work with at first.

Cricut Fabric Coasters

Fabric coasters with a Cricut maker are great, and they need only a few supplies.

These include the maker itself, cotton fabric, fusible fleece, a rotary cutting mat or some scissors, a sewing machine, and an iron.

Cut the fabric to about 12" to fit the cutting mat, if it's longer, you can hang it off, just be careful.

Resize it to about 5" wide. Press Make it, and you'll want to make sure you create four copies.

Press Continue, and then choose medium fabrics similar to cotton. You then load the mat and cut, and then you do it again with the fusible fleece on the cutting mat, changing it to 4.75".

This time, when choosing the material, go to more, and then select fusible fleece.

Cut the fusible fleece, and then attach these to the heart's back with the iron and repeat with the second.

Clip the curves, turn it inside out, and then fold in the edges and stitch it. There you go, a fusible fleece heart coaster.

It's a little bit more complicated, but it's worth trying out.

Difficult Projects

Giant Vinyl Stencils

Vinyl stencils are a good thing to create, too, but they can be hard. Big vinyl stencils make for an excellent Cricut project, and you can use them in various places, including bedrooms for kids.

You only need the explore Air 2, the vinyl that works for it, a pallet, sander, and, of course, paint and brushes.

The first step is preparing the pallet for painting or whatever surface you plan on using this for.

From here, you create the mermaid tail (or any other large image) in Design Space.

Now, you'll learn immediately that big pieces are hard to cut and impossible to do all at once in Design Space.

What you do is section each design accordingly and remove any middle pieces.

Next, you can add square shapes to the image, slicing it into pieces so that it can be cut on a cutting mat that fits.

At this point, you cut out the design by pressing make it, choosing your material, and working in sections.

From here, you put it on the surface that you're using, piecing this together with each line, and you should have one image after piecing it all together.

Then, draw out the line on vinyl, and then paint the initial design. For the second set of stencils, you can simply trace the first one and then paint the inside of them.

At this point, you should have the design finished.

When done, remove it very carefully. And there you have it!

Bigger stencils can be a bit of a project since it involves trying to use multiple designs all at once, but with the right care and the right designs, you'll be able to create whatever it is you need to in Design Space so you can get the results you're looking for.

CHAPTER 5

BEFORE STARTING

Materials

The machines can use many different materials for any project you desire, and we will be breaking down what machine can use which materials. Something that you should know is that there are materials that the Maker can cut than the other machines cannot. Over one hundred different types of fabric, as a matter of fact. The official website of the Cricut machines does change periodically in what they say the machines can cut, and so you will need to check their website as a result of this. In doing so, you will realize what you can still cut and what may have been taken off of the list.

As we have stated in the chapter above, there are four different machines and two different series. The Explore series and the Maker series. The Explore series can only cut certain items, and we are going to list them now.

The Explore series can cut these items:

- Tattoo paper
- Washi tape
- Paint chips
- Wax paper
- Faux suede
- Wrapping paper
- Washi paper
- Poster board
- Parchment paper
- Sticker paper
- Construction paper
- Photo paper
- Printable fabric
- Magnetic sheets
- Paper grocery bags
- Craft foam
- Window cling vinyl
- Cardstock
- Flannel
- Vellum

- Duck cloth
- Wool felt
- Cork board
- Tissue paper
- Duct tape
- Matte vinyl
- Iron-on vinyl
- Leather up to 2.0 mm thick
- Sheet duct tape
- Oil cloth
- Soda cans
- Stencil film
- Glitter foam
- Metallic vellum
- Burlap
- Transparency film
- Chipboard that is up to 2.0 mm thick
- Aluminum metal that is up to .14 mm thick
- Stencil vinyl
- Glitter vinyl
- Glossy vinyl
- Faux leather up to 1.0 mm thick

Fabrics, when used with the Explore series, need to be stabilized with Heat N Bond. Examples of fabrics are shown on the list below:

- Denim
- Felt
- Silk
- Polyester

Other items that the Explore Series can cut will be listed below:

- Chalkboard vinyl
- Adhesive vinyl
- Aluminum foil
- Cardboard
- Stencil film
- Dry erase vinyl
- Printable vinyl
- Outdoor vinyl
- Wood birch up to .5 mm thick
- Cardboard that is corrugated
- Shrink plastic
- Metallic vellum
- White core
- Rice paper
- Photo framing mat
- Pearl cardstock
- Cereal boxes
- Freezer paper

- Iron-on

- Printable iron-on

- Glitter iron-on

- Foil iron-on

- Foil embossed paper

- Neon iron-on

- Matte iron-on

The Maker can cut everything that the Explore series can cut, but it can cut so much more because the Explore series operates with three blades, but the Maker has six. The fact that they have six blades can cut more fabric and thicker fabric. They also differ from the Explore series because the Maker doesn't have to use Heat N Bond to stabilize fabrics.

The Maker is also able to utilize the rotary blade as well. This type of blade is new, and it differs from the others that the Explore machines use because this blade spins and twists with a gliding and rolling motion. This rolling action will allow the Maker to cut side to side and up and down. Having a blade able to cut in any direction will help you with the ability to craft great projects. The Maker can even cut (up to) three layers of light cotton at the same time. This is great for projects that need uniform cuts.

The Maker can also use the knife blade, which is a more precise option and cuts better than the others before it. This blade can cut up to 2.4 mm thick. This machine is also able to use ten times more power to cut than the others as well.

With that being said, the Maker can cut over a hundred different fabrics that others can't. We will be supplying a list of some of those fabrics below:

- Waffle cloth
- Jacquard
- Gossamer
- Khaki
- Damask
- Faille
- Heather
- Lycra
- Mesh
- Calico
- Crepe paper
- Gauze
- Interlock knit
- Grocery bag
- Acetate
- Chantilly lace
- Boucle
- Corduroy
- EVA foam
- Tweed
- Tulle
- Moleskin

- Fleece

- Jersey

- Muslin

- Jute

- Terry cloth

- Velvet

- Knits

- Muslin

Remember that this is just scratching the surface of what the Maker can cut. There are many others because the Maker is considered the ultimate machine and the best of the four. The Maker is also great for sewing, and there are hundreds of these projects on Design Space. Having a machine that can have access to these projects, and the ability to cut thicker materials means that you have a machine that opens your crafting skills to a whole new level.

CHAPTER 6

PROJECTS FOR BEGINNERS

Paper Lollipop

Materials needed: "Cricut" cutting machine, light grip mat, patterned cardstock in desired colors, glitter, wooden dowels, and hot glue.

Step 1

Use your "Cricut ID" to log in to the "Design Space" application. Then click on the "New Project" button on the top right corner of the screen to start a new project and view a blank canvas.

Step 2

We will be using an already existing project from the "Cricut" library and customizing it. So, click on the "Projects" icon and type in "paper lollipop" in the search bar.

Step 3

Click on "Customize" so you can further edit this project to your preference.

Step 4

Once you have altered the design to your satisfaction, it is ready to be cut. Simply click on the "Make It" button on the top right corner of the screen to view the required mats and material for your project.

Step 5

Load the cardstock to your "Cricut" cutting machine and click "Continue" at the bottom right corner of the screen to start cutting your design.

Note: If images and/or fonts used for your design are not free and available for purchase only, then the "Continue" button will not appear, and instead, a "Purchase" button will be visible. Once you have paid for the image or font, the "Continue" button will be available to you.

Step 6

Connect your "Cricut" device to your computer and place the cardstock on top of the cutting mat and load it into the "Cricut" machine by pushing against the rollers. The "Load/Unload" button would already be flashing, so just press that button first, followed by the flashing "Go" button.

Step 7

Use the hot glue to adhere the wooden dowels between the lollipop circles. Then brush the tops with the craft glue and sprinkle on the glitter, as shown in the picture below.

Ornaments

These paper adornments can be tweaked in various manners. An essential thought is to choose the number of layers you'd prefer to utilize. In my model, I utilized 5 layers. However, you can attempt three or even 6... Play with the hope to see which you like best.

Materials:

- Cricut Machine and Cricut Design Space
- Ornament SVG cut document.
- White cardstock
- Glue
- Twine

Cut lovely plans with your Cricut.

Guidelines:

1. Upload the trimming cut record to Cricut Design Space.
2. Ungroup and resize the beautiful layer you'd prefer to utilize. Make a point to set the scoreline to SCORE in Design Space.
3. Send the structure to the tangle. Alter the cut amount to cut 5 duplicates of the structure. Organize on the tangle any way you'd like.
4. Fold each cut structure along the scoreline.
5. Apply the paste to the other side of a cut shape. Line up the subsequent cut shape, press, and hold set up to follow together.
6. Applying the twine: You have two alternatives for applying twine to your trimming.
7. You can wrap and tie the twine around the highest point of the trimming at the neck of the ball shape.
8. You can add a length of twine to the focal point of your adornment before sticking the last different sides together. In the event that you pick this strategy, try to make a bunch at the top and base of the twine, so the twine doesn't sneak out of the focal point of the decoration.

Greeting Cards

Many people buy their first Cricut Maker with the idea of making greeting cards. If you look on Etsy, you will see dozens of people selling home-made cards and earning extra money using their Cricut Maker to make these cards. Many users recommend a Cricut Access Membership. This will give you access to thousands of images, hundreds of fonts, and discounts off purchases for supplies and accessories.

CHAPTER 7

PROJECTS FOR BEGINNERS WITH PAPER

It is ideal to start your first project using paper-based designs since these projects are easier to not only design but also to cut, regardless of the kind of Cricut cutting machine being used. You can get professional-looking results without investing a whole lot of time and money. You will learn to create various projects that you can further customize as you follow the instructions below and have unique designs of your own.

Recipe Stickers

Materials needed: Cricut cutting machine, sticker paper, and cutting mat.

Step 1

Use your Cricut ID to log in to the Design Space application. Then click on the "New Project" button on the top right corner of the screen to start a new project and view a blank canvas.

Step 2

Click on the "Images" icon on the Design Panel and type in "recipe stickers" in the search bar. Select the image that works for you, then click on the "Insert Images" button at the bottom of the screen, as shown in the picture below.

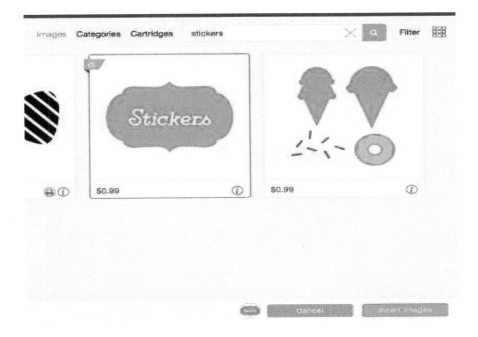

Step 3

The image that you have selected will appear on the canvas and can be edited to your preference. You will be able to make all kinds of changes, for example, changing the color and size of the image (sticker should be between 2-4 inches wide). The image selected for this project has the word "stickers" inside the design, so let's delete that by first clicking on the "Ungroup" button and selecting the "Stickers" layer, and clicking on the red "x" button. Click on the "Text" button and add your recipe's name, as shown in the picture below.

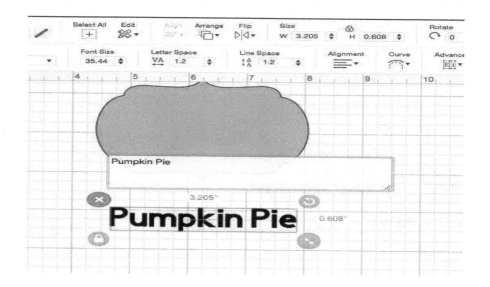

Step 4

Now, move the text to the middle of the design and select the entire design, including the text. Then click on "Align" and select "Center Horizontally", or "Center Vertically", so that your text will be uniformly aligned right in the center of the design.

Step 5

Select all the layers of the design and click on the "Group" icon on the top right of the screen under the Layers Panel. Now, copy and paste the designs and update the text for all your recipes, as shown in the picture below. (**Tip:** You can use your keyboard shortcuts like Ctrl +

C (to copy), and Ctrl + V (to paste) instead of selecting the image and clicking on "Edit" from the Edit bar to view the dropdown option for Copy and Paste.)

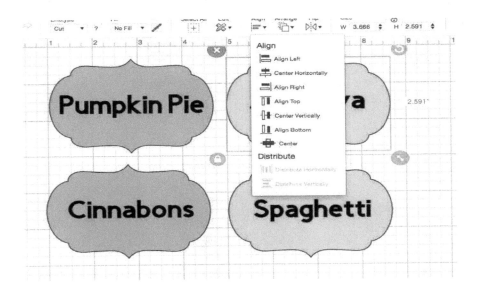

Step 6

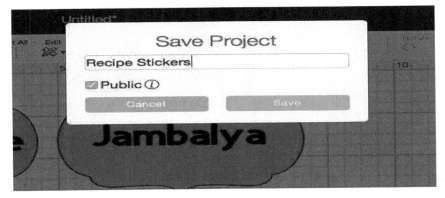

Step 7

Your design is ready to be cut. Simply click on the "Make It" button on the top right corner of the screen. All the required mats and materials will be displayed on the screen. (Tip: You can move your design on the mat by simply dragging and dropping it anywhere on the mat to resemble the cutting space for your material on the actual cutting mat.)

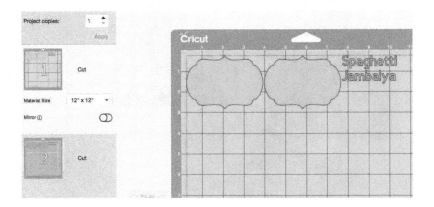

Step 8

Once you have loaded the sticker paper to your Cricut cutting machine, click "Continue" at the bottom right corner of the screen to start cutting your design.

Note: If images and/or fonts used for your design are not free and available for purchase only, then the "Continue" button will not appear, and instead, a "Purchase" button will be visible. Once you have paid for the image or font, the "Continue" button will be available to you.

Step 9

Once your Cricut device has been connected to your computer, set the cut setting to "Vinyl" (recommended to cut the sticker paper since it tends to be thicker than regular paper). Place the sticker paper on top of the cutting mat and load it into the Cricut device by pushing it against the rollers. The "Load/Unload" button would already be flashing, so just press that button first, followed by the flashing "Go" button.

Wedding Invitations

Materials needed: Cricut cutting machine, cutting mat, and cardstock, or your choice of decorative paper/crepe paper/fabric, home printer (if not using Cricut Maker).

Step 1

Use your Cricut ID to log in to the Design Space application. Then click on the "New Project" button on the top right corner of the screen to start a new project and view a blank canvas.

Step 2

A beginner-friendly way to create wedding invitations is a customization of an already existing project from the Design Space library that aligns with your ideas. Click on the "Projects" icon on the Design Panel, then select "Cards" from the "All Categories" drop-down. Enter the keywords "wedding invite" in the search bar.

Step 3

You can click on the project to preview its description and requirements. Once you have found the project, you want to use, click "Customize" at the bottom of the screen so you can edit the invite and add the required text to it.

Step 4

The design will be loaded onto the canvas. Click on the "Text" button and type in the details for your invite. You will modify the font, color, and alignment of the text from the Edit Text Bar on top of the screen. You can even adjust the size of the entire design as needed. (An invitation card can be anywhere from 6 to 9" wide.)

Note: Most cards will require you to change the "Fill" to "Print" on the top of the screen so you can first print then cut the invitation.

Step 5

Select the entire design and click on the "Group" icon on the screen's top right under the Layers Panel. Then click on the "Save" button to enter a name for your project and click "Save" again.

Step 6

Your design can now be printed then cut. Simply click on the "Make It" button on the top right corner of the screen to view the required mats and material. Then use your home printer to print the design on your chosen material (white cardstock or paper), or if using the Cricut Maker, then just follow the prompts on the Design Space application.

Tip: Calibrate your machine first for the "Print then Cut" project by clicking on the hamburger icon next to the "Canvas" ☰ Canvas on the top left of the screen and follow the prompts on the screen, as shown in the picture below.

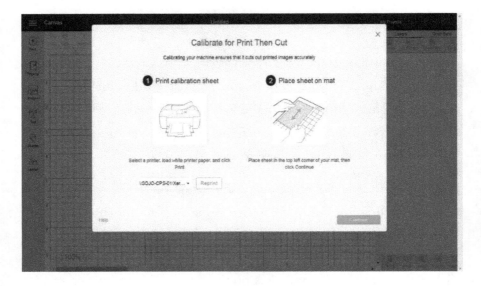

Step 7

Load the material with printed design to your Cricut cutting machine and click "Continue" at the bottom right corner of the screen to start cutting your design.

Note: If images and fonts used for your design are not free and available for purchase only, then the "Continue" button will not appear, and instead, a "Purchase" button will be visible. Once you have paid for the image or font, the "Continue" button will be available to you.

Step 8

Once your Cricut device has been connected to your computer, set the cut setting to "cardstock." Then place the printed cardstock on top of the cutting mat and load it into the Cricut device by pushing against the rollers. The "Load/Unload" button would already be flashing, so just press that button first, followed by the flashing "Go" button. Voilá! You have your wedding invitations all ready to be put in an envelope and on their way to all your wedding guests.

Custom Notebooks

Materials needed: Cricut cutting machine, cutting mat, and washi sheets or your choice of decorative paper/crepe paper/fabric.

Step 1

Use your Cricut ID to log in to the Design Space application. Then click on the "New Project" button on the top right corner of the screen to start a new project and view a blank canvas.

Step 2

Let's use an already existing project from the Cricut library for this. Click on the "Projects" icon on the Design Panel and type in "notebook" in the search bar.

You can view all the projects available by clicking on them, and a pop-up window displaying all the details of the project will appear on your screen.

Step 3

Select the project that you like and click on "Customize" so you can further edit this project to your preference.

Step 4

The selected project will be displayed on the Canvas. You can check from the "Layers Panel" if your design contains only one layer, which is very easy to modify, or multiple layers that can be selectively modified. Click on the Linetype Swatch to view the color palette and select the desired color for your design.

Step 5

Once you have modified the design to your satisfaction, it is ready to be cut. Simply click on the "Make It" button on the top right corner of the screen to view the required mats and material for your project.

Step 6

Load the washi paper sheet to your Cricut cutting machine and click "Continue" at the bottom right corner of the screen to start cutting your design.

Note: If images and fonts used for your design are not free and available for purchase only, then the "Continue" button will not appear, and instead, a "Purchase" button will be visible. Once you have paid for the image or font, the "Continue" button will be available to you.

Step 7

Connect your Cricut device to your computer, and place the washi paper or your chosen paper on top of the cutting mat, and load it into the Cricut machine by pushing against the rollers. The "Load/Unload" button would already be flashing, so just press that button first, followed by the flashing "Go" button. Voilá! Your kids can now enjoy their uniquely customized notebook.

Paper Flowers

Materials needed: Cricut cutting machine, cutting mat, cardstock, and adhesive.

Step 1

Use your Cricut ID to log in to the Design Space application. Then click on the "New Project" button on the top right corner of the screen to start a new project and view a blank canvas.

Step 2

Click on the "Images" icon on the Design Panel and type in "flower" in the search bar. Then select the image you like and click on the "Insert Images" button at the bottom of the screen.

Step 3

The selected image will be displayed on the canvas and edited using applicable tools from the Edit Image Bar. Then copy and paste the flower five times, and make them a size smaller than the preceding flower to create a variable size for depth and texture for the design. Click on the "Linetype Swatch" to view the color palette, and select the desired color for your design.

Step 5

Once you have modified the design to your satisfaction, it is ready to be cut. Simply click on the "Make It" button on the top right corner of the screen to view the required mats and material for your project.

Step 6

Load the cardstock to your Cricut cutting machine and click "Continue" at the bottom right corner of the screen to start cutting your design.

Note: If images and fonts used for your design are not free and available for purchasing only, then the "Continue" button will not appear, and instead, a "Purchase" button will be visible. Once you have paid for the image or font, the "Continue" button will be available to you.

Step 7

Connect your Cricut device to your computer and place the cardstock or your chosen paper on top of the cutting mat and load it into the Cricut machine by pushing against the rollers. The "Load/Unload" button would already be flashing, so just press that button first, followed by the flashing "Go" button.

Step 8

Once the design has been cut, simply remove the cut flowers, and bend them at the center. Then using the adhesive, stack the flowers with the largest flower at the bottom.

CHAPTER 8

PROJECTS FOR BEGINNERS
WITH FABRIC

Tassels

Tassels have almost endless uses. These are incredibly easy to make and can be customized to fit whatever purpose you want. Add them to the edges of pillows or blankets, hang them from a string to make a banner, use one as a keychain or zipper pull, and a million other things! You can also try making these with leather or faux leather for a classier look. Tassels are cute on just about everything. For best results, use your Cricut Maker for this project.

Materials:

- 12" x 18" fabric rectangles
- Fabric mat
- Glue gun

Instructions:

1. Open Cricut Design Space and create a new project.

2. Select the "Image" button in the lower left-hand corner and search "tassel."

3. Select the image of a rectangle with lines on each side and click "Insert."

4. Place the fabric on the cutting mat.

5. Send the design to the Cricut.

6. Remove the fabric from the mat, saving the extra square.

7. Place the fabric face down and begin rolling tightly, starting on the uncut side. Untangle the fringe as needed.

8. Use some of the scrap fabric and a hot glue gun to secure the tassel at the top.

9. Decorate whatever you want with your new tassels!

Monogrammed Drawstring Bag

Drawstring bags are quick and easy to use. They're just as easy to make! This includes steps for sewing the pieces together, but you could even use fabric glue if you're not great with a needle and thread. You can keep these bags handy for every member of your family to grab and go as needed. You can tell them apart with the monograms, or use a different design on each one to customize them to a certain use, or just decorate it. You can even use these as gift bags! This project uses heat transfer vinyl for the designs, so you'll need your Cricut EasyPress or iron. For best results, use your Cricut Maker for this project.

Materials:

- Two matching rectangles of fabric
- Needle and thread
- Ribbon
- Heat transfer vinyl
- Cricut EasyPress or iron
- Cutting mat
- Weeding tool or pick

Instructions:

1. Open Cricut Design Space and create a new project.
2. Select the "Image" button in the lower left-hand corner and search "monogram."
3. Select the monogram of your choice and click "Insert."
4. Place the iron-on material shiny liner side down on the cutting mat.

5. Send the design to the Cricut.

6. Use the weeding tool or pick to remove excess material.

7. Remove the monogram from the mat.

8. Center the monogram on your fabric, then move it a couple of inches down so that it won't be folded up when the ribbon is drawn.

9. Iron the design onto the fabric.

10. Place the two rectangles together, with the outer side of the fabric facing inward. Sew around the edges, leaving a seam allowance. Leave the top open and stop a couple of inches down from the top.

11. Fold the top of the bag down until you reach your stitches.

12. Sew along the bottom of the folded edge, leaving the sides open.

13. Turn the bag right side out.

14. Thread the ribbon through the loop around the top of the bag.

15. Use your new drawstring bag to carry what you need!

Print Socks

Socks are the ultimate cozy item. No warm pajamas are complete without a pair! Add a cute, hidden accent to the bottom of your or your child's socks with little paw prints. For the easiest read, make sure the sock color and vinyl color contrast. Or make them in the same color for a hidden design! The shine of the vinyl will stand out from the cloth in certain lights. Since this uses heat transfer vinyl, you'll need your Cricut EasyPress or iron. You can use the Cricut Explore One, Cricut Air 2, or Cricut Maker for this project.

Materials:

- Socks
- Heat transfer vinyl
- Cutting mat
- Scrap cardboard
- Weeding tool or pick
- Cricut EasyPress or iron

Instructions:

1. Open Cricut Design Space and create a new project.
2. Select the "Image" button in the lower left-hand corner and search "paw prints."
3. Select the paw prints of your choice and click "Insert."
4. Place the iron-on material on the mat.
5. Send the design to the Cricut.
6. Use the weeding tool or pick to remove excess material.
7. Remove the material from the mat.
8. Fit the scrap cardboard inside of the socks.
9. Place the iron-on material on the bottom of the socks.
10. Use the EasyPress to adhere it to the iron-on material.
11. After cooling, remove the cardboard from the socks.
12. Wear your cute paw print socks!

Night Sky Pillow

The night sky is a beautiful thing, and you will love having a piece of it on a cozy pillow. Customize this with the stars you love most, or add constellations, planets, galaxies, and more! Adults and children alike can enjoy these lovely pillows. A sewing machine will make this project a breeze to put together, or you can use a needle and thread. If you're not great at sewing, use fabric glue to close the pillow. Choose a soft fabric that you love so that you can cuddle up with this pillow. You will need your Cricut EasyPress or iron to attach the heat transfer vinyl. You can use the Cricut Explore One, Cricut Explore Air 2, or Cricut Maker for this project.

Materials:

- Black, dark blue, or dark purple fabric
- Heat transfer vinyl in gold or silver
- Cutting mat
- Polyester batting
- Weeding tool or pick
- Cricut EasyPress

Instructions:

1. Decide the shape you want for your pillow and cut two matching shapes out of the fabric.

2. Open Cricut Design Space and create a new project.

3. Select the "Image" button in the lower left-hand corner and search "stars."

4. Select the stars of your choice and click "Insert."

5. Place the iron-on material on the mat.

6. Send the design to the Cricut.

7. Use the weeding tool or pick to remove excess material.

8. Remove the material from the mat.

9. Place the iron-on material on the fabric.

10. Use the EasyPress to adhere it to the iron-on material. Sew the two fabric pieces together, leaving an allowance for a seam and a small space. Fill the pillow with polyester batting through the small open space.

11. Sew the pillow shut.

12. Cuddle up to your starry pillow!

Clutch Purse

Clutches are an incredibly useful thing to have around. It is smaller than a regular purse, yet big enough to hold what you need, and you can use them for any occasion. Create a few of these in different colors and patterns to match different outfits! This clutch is inspired by a project that Cricut has in the Design Space. It is the most advanced of the fabric projects in this book, and it uses the most sewing. For the best results, use the Cricut Maker for this project.

Materials:

- Two fabrics, one for the exterior and one for the interior
- Fusible fleece
- Fabric cutting mat
- D-ring
- Sew-on snap
- Lace
- Zipper
- Sewing machine
- Fabric scissors
- Keychain or charm of your choice

Instructions:

1. Open Cricut Design Space and create a new project.
2. Select the "Image" button in the lower left-hand corner and search for "essential wallet."
3. Select the essential wallet template and click "Insert."
4. Place the fabric on the mat.
5. Send the design to the Cricut.
6. Remove the fabric from the mat.
7. Attach the fusible fleecing to the wrong side of the exterior fabric.
8. Attach lace to the edges of the exterior fabric.
9. Assemble the D-ring strap.
10. Place the D-ring onto the strap and sew it into place.

11. Fold the pocket pieces' wrong side out over the top of the zipper and sew it into place.

12. Fold the pocket's wrong side in and sew the sides.

13. Sew the snap in the pocket.

14. Lay the pocket on the right side of the main fabric lining so that the corners of the pocket's bottom are behind the curved edges of the lining fabric. Sew the lining piece to the zipper tape.

15. Fold the lining behind the pocket and iron in place.

16. Sew on the other side of the snap.

17. Trim the zipper so that it's not overhanging the edge.

18. Sew the two pocket layers to the exterior fabric across the bottom.

19. Sew around all of the layers.

20. Trim the edges with fabric scissors.

21. Turn the clutch almost completely inside out and sew the opening closed.

22. Turn the clutch inside out and press the corners into place.

23. Attach your charm or keychain to the zipper.

24. Carry your new clutch wherever you need it!

CHAPTER 9

PROJECTS FOR BEGINNERS WITH CLOTHING

Custom Graphic T-shirt

First, you will need to determine what you want your T-shirt to say. It is best to stick with just one color when you start. But as you get better at creating with your Cricut, you can move on to more color options in one design. Next is to pick which T-shirt you would like to use. This can be a preexisting shirt from your closet, or it could be one that you purchased specifically for this project. The T-shirt needs to be a material that can be ironed.

Supplies Needed:

- The Cricut machine
- Vinyl for the letters
- Your Cricut tools kit

I will walk you step-by-step on how you will make this vinyl lettering T-shirt.

1. Start by choosing the image you want to use. This can be done in Photoshop, or you can place your text directly into the Design Space.

2. Next, open the Cricut Design Space. Choose the canvas you wish to use by clicking the Canvas icon on the dashboard located on the left-hand side. Select the canvas that you will be using for your vinyl letters. This can be anything within the categories they offer.

3. Then, select the size of the T-shirt for the canvas. This is located on the right-hand side of the options.

4. Now, click Upload for uploading your image, which is located on the left-hand side. Select the image you are using by browsing the list of images in your file library. Then select the type of image that you have picked. For most projects, especially iron-on ones, you will select the Simple Cut option.

81

5. Click on the white space that you want to be removed by cutting out. Remember to cut the insides of every letter.

6. Next, be super diligent, and press "Cut Image" instead of "Print" first. You do not want to print the image simply. You cut it as well.

7. Place the image on your chosen canvas and adjust the sizing of the image.

8. Place your iron-on image with the vinyl side facing down on the mat, and then turn the dial to the setting for iron-on.

9. Next, you will want to click the Mirror Image setting for the image before hitting go.

10. Once you have cut the image, you should remove the excess vinyl from the edges around the lettering or image. Then use the tool for weeding out the inner pieces of the letters.

11. Now you will be placing the vinyl on the T-shirt.

12. And now, the fun part begins. You will get to iron the image on the T-shirt. Using the cotton setting, you will need to use the hottest setting to get your iron. There should not be any steam.

13. You want to warm the T-shirt by placing the iron on the shirt portion to hold the image. This should be warmed up for 15 seconds.

14. Next, lay the vinyl out exactly where you want it to be placed. Place a pressing cloth over the top of the plastic. This will prevent the plastic on the shirt from melting.

15. Place your iron onto the pressing cloth for around 30 seconds. Flip the T-shirt, and place the pressing cloth and iron on the backside of the vinyl.

16. Flip your T-shirt back over and begin to peel off the sticky part of the vinyl that you have been overlaying on the shirt. This will separate the vinyl from the plastic backing. This should be done while the plastic and vinyl are hot. Then proceed to pull up, and it should come off nicely.

17. This should remove the plastic from the vinyl that is now on the T-shirt. Place the pressing cloth on top of the vinyl once again and heat it to ensure that it is good and stuck.

18. Although there are tons of steps, it is still an amazingly simple process.

Halloween T-Shirt

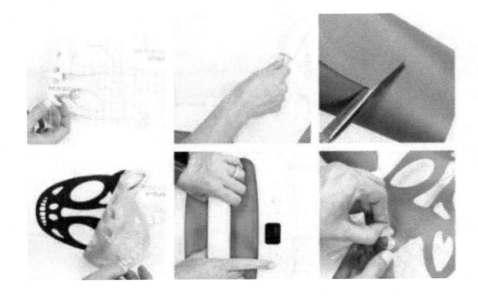

Materials Needed:

- T-shirt Blanks

- Glam Halloween SVG Files

- Cardstock

- Transfer Sheets (Black and Pink)

- Butcher Paper (comes with Infusible Ink rolls)

- LightGrip Mat

- EasyPress (12" x 10" size recommended)

- EasyPress Mat

- Lint Roller

STEPS:

1. Import the SVG files into Cricut Design Space, and arrange them as you want them on the T-shirt.

2. Change the sizes of the designs to get them to fit on the T-shirt.

3. Using the slice tool, slice the pink band away from the hat's bowler part (the largest piece). Make a copy of this band, and then slice it from the lower part of the hat. With these done, you will have three pieces that fit together.

4. You can change the designs' colors as you would like them. When you are done with the preparation, click "Make It."

5. Ensure that you invert your image using the "Mirror" toggle. This is even more important if there is text on your design, as infusible ink designs should be done in inverse. This is because the part with the ink is to go right on the destination material.

6. Click on "Continue"

7. **For the material:** Select Infusible ink. After this, cut the design out using your Cricut Machine.

8. With the designs cut out, weed the transfer sheet.

9. Cut around the designs such that the transfer tape does not cover any part of the infusible ink sheet. Make sure that this is done well, as any part of the infusible ink that is not in contact with the fabric will not be transferred.

10. Preheat your EasyPress to 385 degrees and set your EasyPress mat.

11. Prepare your T-shirt by placing it on the EasyPress mat, then using a lint roller to remove any lint from the front.

12. Insert the Cardstock in the t-shirt, between the front and back, just where the design will be. This will protect the other side of the T-shirt from having the Infusible Ink on it.

13. If necessary, use the lint roller on the T-shirt again, after which you should heat your shirt with the EasyPress. Do this at 385 degrees for 15 seconds.

14. Turn the part where the design faces on the T-shirt. Place the butcher paper on the design, ensuring, again, that the backing does not overlap the design.

15. Place the EasyPress over the design and hold it in place for 40 seconds. Do not move the EasyPress around so that your design does not end up looking smudged.

16. Remove the EasyPress from the shirt and remove the transfer sheet.

17. To layer colors, ensure that your cutting around the transfer sheet is done as close as possible, then repeat the previous three steps for each color. This will prevent the transfer sheet from removing part of the color on the previously transferred design.

'Queen B' T-shirt

Supplies Needed:

- Plain cotton T-shirt in the color of your choice
- Iron-on vinyl, also called heat transfer vinyl (HTV, gold)
- Green Standard Grip mat
- Cricut Fine-Point Blade
- Weeding tool
- Pair of scissors for cutting the material to size
- Brayer

- Iron or the Cricut EasyPress Iron
- Cricut heat press mat to iron on

Instructions:

1. Start a new project in Design Space.
2. Choose 'Templates' from the left-hand side menu.
3. Choose the 'Classic T-shirts' template.
4. From the top menu, choose the type of T-shirt; kids' short sleeve.
5. From the top menu, choose the size of the T-shirt; small.
6. The back and the front of the T-shirt will appear on Design Space in the workspace.
7. From the top menu, select the color of the T-shirt you are using; pink.
8. Select 'Text' from the left-hand menu and type in 'Queen B.'
9. Set the font; a great free font for this project is Bauhaus 9.
10. Position the text on the T-shirt, then set the size and change the color to gold.
11. Choose images and find a bee picture. There is a nice free image or some really cute images you can buy.
12. Position the bee above the B and set the color to gold. You can rotate it into a tilted position.
13. Click on the 'Make it' button, and you will be prompted with another screen showing the design on the cutting board. This is because, for iron-on vinyl, you need to mirror the image. You mirror the image in order to iron it on with the correct side up. Click the 'Mirror' button on the left-hand side of the screen.

You will see your writing and image look like it is back-to-front. You may want to move the bee over a bit, giving a bit of space between the image and writing.

14. Reset your dial on the Cricut to 'Custom.'
15. In Design Space, choose the everyday iron-on for your material setting.
16. You can set the pressure to a bit more if you like.
17. You will see a warning letting you know that mirroring must be ON for iron-on vinyl. It reminds you to place the vinyl facedown as well.
18. Check that you have the fine-point blade loaded in 'Cartridge Two' of the Cricut. Nothing is needed for cartridge one.
19. Cut the vinyl to the space that is indicated by the Cricut Design Space.
20. Place the shiny side of the iron-on vinyl down onto the cutting mat. Use your brayer to smooth out the vinyl onto your mat.
21. Load the cutting into the Cricut, and when the Cricut is ready, click 'Go' for it to cut.
22. Unload the cutting mat when it has been cut. Remove the design from the mat, and gently remove the mat side of the vinyl from the carrier sheet (matte side of the vinyl).
23. Use the weeding tool to pick out the areas of the letters like the middles of the B.
24. Place your T-shirt onto the Cricut pressing mat with the middle section you want the transfer.

25. If you are using the Cricut EasyPress, you can go to the Cricut website to find the heat transfer guide and the settings you will need for the press. Follow the instructions with the Cricut EasyPress.

26. For a normal iron, preheat the iron.

27. Place the Cricut heat press mat inside the shirt.

28. Heat the surface of the T-shirt for 5 seconds with the iron.

29. Put the design on the shirt where it is to be ironed on with the carrier sheet up.

30. Place a parchment sheet over the vinyl to protect the iron and the design.

31. Place the iron on the design and hold the iron in place on the design, applying a bit of pressure for up to 0 seconds.

32. Turn the T-shirt inside out, and place the iron on the back of the design for another 0 seconds.

33. When it is done, turn the T-shirt right side out and gently pull the carrier sheet off.

34. Do not wash the T-shirt for a few hours after the transfer has been done.

CHAPTER 10

PROJECTS FOR BEGINNERS WITH GLASS

Window decoration

Necessary material: "Cricut Maker" or "Cricut Explore," cutting mat, orange window sticker (non-adhesive material that has static adhesion so it can be easily applied to glass; as it has no sticky adhesion like vinyl, be sure to wear it sideways inside the window to protect the exposure from the elements).

Step 1

To start a new project, after logging into your "Cricut" account at "Design Space," click the "New Project" button in the upper right corner of the screen, and a blank canvas will appear.

Step 2

Let's use an existing project from the "Cricut" library and customize it. Then click the "Projects" icon in the "Design Panel" and click the "All Categories" drop-down menu to view all existing projects that you can select from. For this example, we will click on "Home Decor," then type "window" in the search bar to narrow the search to window cling projects.

You can view all available projects by clicking on them, and a pop-up window will appear on the screen with all project details.

Step 3

The project selected for this example is shown in the image below. Click "Customize" at the bottom of the screen so you can change the design as desired.

hare   ☆ 3916

Happy Halloween Window Cling

Easy | Less Than 30 Minutes   Happy Hall

Step 4

The selected design will appear on the canvas. You can see in the "Layers Panel" that this drawing contains multiple layers, but the two lower layers are hidden by the canvas and will be excluded from the cut. You can change the drawing color by clicking "Linetype Swatch" to display the color palette and select the desired color, as below screenshot shown.

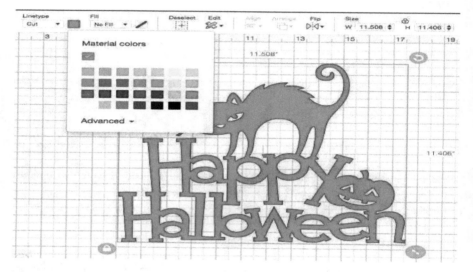

Step 5

The design is ready to be printed and cut. Just click the "Make It" button in the upper right corner of the screen. You will see the required mats and material displayed on the screen.

Step 6

Load the orange window attached to your "Cricut" machine and click "Continue" in the lower right corner of the screen to start cutting your design.

Note: The "Continue" button will not appear if you have used images and fonts for the design that are not free and only available for purchase. Instead, a "Buy" will appear at the bottom right of the screen so that you can purchase the image or font first, and once you've made your purchase, the "Continue" button will be available to you.

Step 7

Once the "Cricut" device has been connected to your computer, set the cutting set to "Vinyl." We recommend using this setting for cutting sticky paper as it tends to be thicker than plain paper. Place the sticky paper on top of the cutting mat, and load it into the "Cricut" device by pressing against the rollers. The "Load / Unload" button will start flashing, so press it. Then press the "Go" button, which would already be flashing. Voilá! You have window decorations ready for Halloween.

Wine glass decoration

Necessary material: "Cricut Maker" or "Cricut Explore," cutting mat, vinyl (gold), transfer tape, scrapper, wine glasses.

Step 1

To start a new project, after logging into your "Cricut" account at "Design Space," click the "New Project" button in the upper right corner of the screen, and a blank canvas will appear.

Step 2

Let's use text for this project. Click "Text" from the "Designs Panel" on the left of the screen and type "WINE o'clock" or any other phrase you like.

Step 3

For the image below, the "Anna's Fancy Lettering - Hannah" font in purple has been selected, as shown in the image below. But you can let your creativity take over this step and choose any color or font you like. Select and copy-paste your image for the number of times you want to print your design.

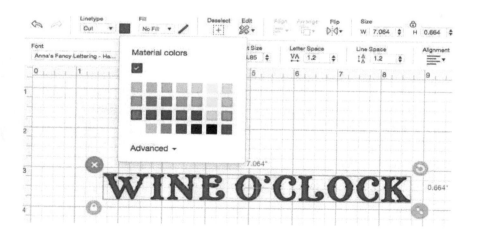

Step 4

Click "Save" in the upper right corner of the screen and name the project as desired, for example, "Wineglass Decoration" and click "Save."

Step 5

The design is ready to be cut. Just click the "Make It" button in the upper right corner of the screen. You will see the required mats and material displayed on the screen, as shown in the image below.

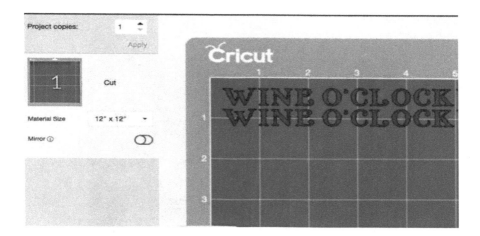

Step 6

Load the vinyl onto your "Cricut" machine and click "Continue" in the lower right corner of the screen to start cutting your design.

Step 7

Connect your "Cricut" device to your computer and place the washi paper or paper of your choice on the cutting mat and load it into the "Cricut" machine by pushing against the rollers. The "Load / Unload" button will start flashing, so just press it. Then press the "Go" button, which would already be flashing.

Step 8

Carefully remove the excess vinyl from the sheet. To easily glue your design onto the wine glass without stretching the pieces, place the transfer tape over the cut design. After cleaning the surface, slowly peel the paper backing on the vinyl from one end to the other with a twisting motion to ensure even placement. Now, use the scraper tool on top of the transfer ribbon to remove any bubbles, and then remove the transfer ribbon. Voilá! You have your custom wine glasses, which may look like the image below.

CHAPTER 11

PROJECTS FOR

INTERMEDIATE

Giant Vinyl Stencils

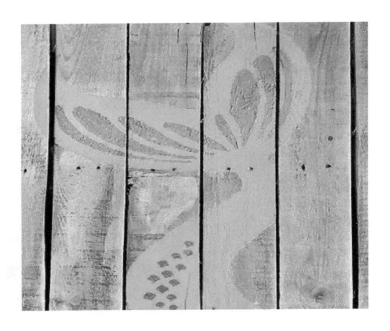

Vinyl stencils are a good thing to create too, but they can be hard. Big vinyl stencils make for an excellent Cricut project, and you can use them in various places, including bedrooms for kids.

You only need the explore Air 2, the vinyl that works for it, a pallet, sander, and of course, paint and brushes. The first step is preparing the pallet for painting, or whatever surface you plan on using this for.

From here, you create the mermaid tail (or any other large image) in Design Space. You will now learn immediately that big pieces are hard to cut and impossible to do all at once in Design Space.

What you do is section each design accordingly, and remove any middle pieces. Next, you can add square shapes to the image, slicing it into pieces to be cut on a cutting mat that fits.

At this point, you cut out the design by pressing 'Make It,' choosing your material, and working in sections.

From here, you put it on the surface that you are using, piecing this together with each line. You should have one image after piecing it all together. Then, draw out the line on vinyl, and then paint the initial design. For the second set of stencils, you can simply trace the first one, and then paint the inside of them. At this point, you should have the design finished. When done, remove it very carefully.

And there you have it! Bigger stencils can be a bit of a project, since it involves trying to use multiple designs all at once; but with the right care and the right designs, you will be able to create whatever it is you need to in Design Space, so you can get the results you are looking for.

Cricut Quilts

Quilts are a bit hard to do for many people, but did you know that you can use Cricut to make it easier? Here, you will learn an awesome project that will help you do this. To begin, you start with the Cricut Design Space. Here, you can add different designs that work for your project. For example, if you are making a baby blanket or quilt with animals on it, you can add little fonts with the names of the animals or different pictures of them too. From here, you want to make sure you choose the option to reverse the design. That way, you will have it printed on correctly. At this point, make your quilt. Do various designs and sew the quilt as you want to.

From here, you should cut it on the iron-on heat transfer vinyl. You can choose that, and then press 'Cut.' The image will then cut into the piece.

At this point, it will cut itself out, and you can proceed to transfer this with some parchment paper. Use an EasyPress for best results and push it down. There you go, an easy addition that will enhance the way your blankets look.

Cricut Unicorn Backpack

If you are making a present for a child, why not give them some cool unicorns? Here is a lovely unicorn backpack you can try to make. To make this, you need ¾ yards of a woven fabric, which is strong since it will help stabilize the backpack. You will also need half a yard of quilting cotton for the lining. The coordinating fabric should be around about an eighth of a yard. You will need: about a yard of fusible interfacing, some strap adjuster rings, a zipper that is about 14" and does not separate, and some stuffing for the horn.

To start, you will want to cut the main fabric; you should use straps, the loops, a handle, some gussets for a zipper, and the bottom and side gussets.

The lining should be done too, and you should make sure you have the interfacing. You can use fusible flex foam to help make it a little bit bulkier.

From here, cut everything and then apply the interfacing to the backside. The flex-foam should be adjusted to achieve the bulkiness you are looking for. You can trim this, too. The interfacing should be on the backside; then, add the flex foam to the main fabric. The adhesive side of this will be on the right-hand side of the interfacing.

Fold the strap pieces in half and push one down on each backside. Halve it, and then press it again; stitch these closer to every edge, and also along the short-pressed edge, as well.

From here, do the same thing with the other side, add the ring for adjustment, and stitch the bottom of these to the back piece's main part.

Then add them both to the bottom.

At this point, you have the earpieces that should have the backside facing out. Stitch, then flip out, and add the pieces.

Add these inner pieces to the outer ear, and then stitch these together.

At this point, you make the unicorn face in the Design Space. You will notice immediately that everything will be black when you use this program, but you can change this by adjusting the desired layers to each color. You can also just use a template that fits, but you should always mirror this before cutting it.

Choose vinyl, and then insert the material onto the cutting mat. From there, cut it and remove the iron-on slowly.

You will need to do this in pieces, which is fine because it allows you to use different colors. Remember to insert the right color for each cut. At this point, add the zipper, and there you go!

20 Custom Back to School Supplies

This tutorial will show you how to use your iPad to create and convert designs for your Cricut machine to cut!

Materials needed:

- Vinyl
- Standard Grip Mat
- White Paper
- Markers (including black)
- Pencil Case
- 3 Ring Binder
- iPad Pro (optional)
- Apple Pencil
- Cricut Design Space App
- Drawing app (e.g., ProCreate)
- Procreate Brushes

Instructions:

1. The first thing to do is convert your kid's drawing into an SVG file that the Cricut Design Space recognizes. This will be done by tracing it in the ProCreate app.

2. Get your child's design: it should not be too complex, to minimize weeding.

3. Open the Procreate app on your iPad.

4. Create a new canvas on ProCreate. Click on the 'Wrench' icon and select 'Image.'

5. Next, click 'Take a Photo.' Take a picture of the design. When you are satisfied with the image, click 'Use It.'

6. On the Layer Panel (the two squares icon), add a new layer by clicking the 'plus' sign.

7. In the layers panel, select the layer containing the picture and click the 'N.' Also, reduce the layer's opacity so that you can easily see your draw lines.

8. From your imported brushes, select the 'Marker' brush. To avoid the need to import a brush, choose the inking brush. You can resize the brush in the brush settings under the 'General' option.

On the new layer, trace over the drawing.

9. Click on the 'Wrench' icon, click 'Share,' then 'PNG.'

10. Next, 'Save' the image to your device.

11. The next stage is to cut the design out in Cricut Design Space

12. Open the Cricut Design Space app on your iPad.

13. Create a 'New Project.'

14. Select 'Upload' (located at the screen's bottom). Select 'Select from Camera Roll' and select the PNG image you created in ProCreate, or the image you traced out.

15. Follow the next steps.

16. Save the design as a cut file and insert it into the canvas. Here, you can resize the design or add other designs.

17. Next, click 'Make It' to send it to your Cricut.

18. Choose 'Vinyl' as the material.

19. Place the vinyl on the mat and use the Cricut to cut it.

20. Now, you can place the vinyl cutouts on the back, to make your child stand out!

Conclusion

Congratulations on making it to the end.

If you are an experienced user, CRICUT® Pro X2 is a great tool for many reasons. However, if you want to take advantage of the advanced features of your CRICUT® Pro X2, you need to upgrade to the PRO version. The tool has many advanced features such as double action blade system, navigation on the tool for precision cutting, scanning function; laser engraving; shadow cutting; ultra-fine detail line control; preset modes and more! This makes CRICUT® Pro X2 even for experienced users!